Thank you so much for taking time to invest in yourself. I am truly excited about the doors that will open for you simply because you are taking the first step, to go beyond the vision board. Some of you possessing this workbook will use these tools to launch multiple business. People are waiting for what you have on the inside to come alive - Books, business of all kinds; ministry, food, health, community centers, shelters, talk shows.

This workbook, along with the seminar, is purposed to empower, equip, and enhance you. It empowers you with the ability to dream bigger. It powerfully equips you with the understanding, tools, and the confidence to move forward with your vision. Lastly, it enhances your business knowledge and takes you to the next level to start earning the money you always wanted to make. Please understand these tools will only work if you invest your time. My hope and desire is that you make your dreams a reality by applying these tools. Come forth! ITS YOUR NOW SEASON! Let's Go. I believe in You!

Best,

Hamiyd Washington, Business Consultant/Coach

PICTURE IT!

PLAN IT

Push it!

PROSPER IN IT

~ H.A.M. WASHINGTON

2

I can control the way you feel and the way you act

I can make you rise and fall

I can work for you or against you

I can make you a success or a failure

I can make you wretched or dejected

I can make you act, work, love and

I can be nurtured to be great and

beautifully seen by others through the action of you

I can make you strong or weak

I can make your heart happy and sing with joy

I can make you believe or not believe

I can make you sick and useless

I can be like a shackle, heavy and attached, burdensome

I can make you handsome and pretty or ugly as only as ugly can be

Or I can make you bright, shiny, fleeting

Lost forever but captured by pen or purpose

I can never be removed, only replaced, I am a thought

Why not get to know me better?

I can be intuitive, intellectual, intentional

I can be inquisitive, inquiring, inscribing

I can be insistent, insolent, insincere

I can be insensitive, insensible, insignificant

I can be an insurgent that is always insulting, I am insurmountable!

I can be humble, thankful, appreciative

I can be approachable, appealing, appraisal

I am appointed, appropriate, approved

I am professional, proficient, projectile

I am prominent, promising, promoted,

"I am prophecy," proscribed, proscription

I am a prospect who shall prosper in prosperity

I am a thought

Why not get to know me better?

~ RASHID RASHAD,
The Power of Family Unity 3

WHAT'S YOUR TYPE OF BUSINESS?

1. IMPORTANCE (What & Why)

_____

_____

_____

2. IDENTITY (Worth)

- STRENGTHS

_____

_____

- WEAKNESSES

_____

_____

3. INVOLVEMENT / INVESTMENT (Work)

_____

_____

_____

4. INFLUENCE (World)

_____

_____

_____

5. IMPLEMENT (When)

_____

_____

First write down your goal; your second job is to breakdown your goal into a series, beginning with steps which are absurdly easy ~Fitzhugh Dodson

The 4 T's

TARGET MARKET

(Audience)

TOUCH THE HEART

(Needs Being Served)

TALENT NEEDED

(Help Wanted)

TREASURE

(Resources)

An idea without execution is creative abortion. ~ +Eugene Smith

BRANDING

What comes to mind when you see these brands?

WRITE down 5 brands you use constantly and why you're loyal.

BRANDS   LOYALTY

1. _____   1. _____

2. _____   2. _____

3. _____   3. _____

4. _____   4. _____

5. _____   5. _____

If opportunity doesn't knock, build the door. ~Milton Berle

WHAT IS A BRAND?

A brand is an image that resides in the mind of the consumer.

There are components that assist in identifying a brand:

- Logo
- Tag Lines
- Color

When you are looking to create a brand, there are many things to take into consideration. You want your brand to stand out above the rest.

Your brand must be:

Appealing!

Appropriate!

Something you *Appreciate!*

Nothing beats genuine interest! – Pastor Richie Patterson, Kind Culture

CREATING YOUR BRAND

To design the right logo, answer the following questions.

1. What does my brand represent?

2. Why will people choose my brand over another?

3. Is my brand targeted or broad?

4. What emotions do you want your brand to radiate?

SEARCHING for The Right Logo

When searching for the right logo, it must speak to who you are, what you represent, and the type of business you are running.

Most people when search for a logo for their brand on the internet. This is a big mistake. Why is it a mistake?

1. Certain logos online are copywritten.
    a. Meaning if used without authorization you may incur court fees.
2. Some other person or business may be using the same logo.
    a. This can compromise the authenticity and integrity of your business.
3. It doesn't really characterize your business.
    a. Your brand must possess appeal. Your brand must speak for you!

One of the biggest lies I tell myself is I don't need to write it down I'll remember it. ~Unknown

TAGLINES

Taglines give a brief explanation of the logo itself. It is a brief description of what you want your consumer to know about your business.

1. Summarize your entire business into one sentence.

2. Slim it down into a catch phrase (no more than 4 words).

Your tagline must create an "Oooooo" experience for the consumer

Overall goal – not tailored to one area

Obligation to the customer - focused

Optimistic – provide hope in the product

Original – it must have you in it

Opportunity – creates accessibility to your business

Operational – create movement

Write the taglines to the following logos on the line below

_____   _____   _____

_____   _____   _____

A picture is worth a thousand words ~Unknown

Let's create a tagline for your business

Summarize your business into one sentence:

_____

_____

Slim down your sentence to one phrase:

" _____ "

Cut it down to three words.

_____ _____ _____

Cut it down to one word.

_____

What makes more sense? Use that as your tagline.

_____
FINALIZE YOUR TAGLINE

The *Attitude* of Color

Colors play a major role in branding, logos, and emblems. Read how color helps sell your business.

PRIMARY COLORS

Fire & Blood: It is associated with energy, war, danger, strength, power, determination as well as passion, desire, and love. It also symbolizes leadership, excitement, youthfulness, and boldness.

Sky & Sea: It is symbolic of depth and stability, trust, loyalty, wisdom, confidence, intelligence, faith, truth, strength, and heaven.

Sunshine: It is commonly related to joy, happiness, intellect, clarity, warmth, optimism, and energy.

SECONDLY COLORS

Nature: It represents growth, health, harmony, freshness, and fertility. Green has a strong emotional correspondence with safety and peacefulness. Dark green is also commonly associated with money.

Optimism: (a fusion of the energy of red and the happiness of yellow) It symbolizes enthusiasm, fascination, friendliness, confidence, cheerfulness, happiness, creativity, social ideas, determination, deliverance, attraction, success, encouragement, and stimulation. It is associated with joy, sunshine, and the tropics.

Royalty: (combines the stability of blue & the energy of red): It symbolizes power, nobility, wisdom, luxury, and ambition. It conveys wealth and extravagance. Purple is associated with dignity, independence, imagination, creativity, mystery, and magic

Earthy, masculinity, ethnicity, simple, dependable

Feminine, candy, sensitive, love, calmness

REFLECTORS of COLOR

Light, goodness, innocence, cleanliness, and purity. It is the color of perfection

Power, elegance, formality, and mystery

Balance, neutral, calmness, old age

Some people dream of success, while other people wake up every morning and make it happen. ~Wayne Huizenga

The *Attitude* of Color

PRIMARY	VENUE	PURPOSE
BLUE	Entertainment, communication, children's products, technology, aerospace, (navy) accounting, health care, security, finance	Draw attention, inspire, stimulate productivity, communicate Consciousness (navy), reduce stress, relax, secure, create order
RED	Entertainment, food, sports, fire protection, children's products	Stimulate, create urgency, caution, encourage
YELLOW	Food, sports, travel, leisure, transportation	Awaken awareness, energize, stimulate, relaxation, affect mood
SECONDARY	VENUE	PURPOSE
GREEN	Environment, education, alternative energy, entertainment (dark green) real estate, farming, nonprofit	Growth, nurture, rejuvenation, possession, encourage
ORANGE	Art, food, sports, transportation, entertainment	Fun, draw attention, express freedom, stimulate
VIOLET / PURPLE	Humanitarian, psychic, belief	Inspiration, intuition, evoke creativity, power, and wisdom, luxury
PINK	Women's products, beauty, fashion	Compulsion, creativity, motivation, action
BROWN	Land, construction, legal, food, transportation	Warmth, common sense, suppression of emotion
REFLECTORS	VENUE	PURPOSE
BLACK	All venues	Hide feeling, create mystery, create fear
GREY	All venues	Timelessness, depressed energy, composed

Your marketing reach is determined by how well you understand color and color your business! ~H A M Washington

PUTTING IT ALL TOGETHER

Type of Business (pg. 4):

_____

Characteristics to Describe You (pg. 8):

_____

_____

Tagline for Business (pg. 10):

_____

Colors for Business (pgs. 11 – 1 2)

_____

HINT:

This is the info you will use to design your logo. You can also forward this information over to a graphic designer* to design for you.

Prices for a graphic designer can range from $50 - $1,000 depending on design of logo.

Write this, write what you see, write it in big block letters so that it can be read on the run...it won't lie. It is on its way, it will come right on time. ~Habakkuk 2:2 MSG

SOCIAL MEDIA

Social Media is a trending term to describe how people today are leveraging various media tools to interact. As this form of communication becomes more and more prevalent today, those who seek a 21st Century Multimillion Dollar success will need to know what these tools are and how to utilize them to expand the consumer reach. Media and video platforms are paving the way for advertisements to source marketing and grow business. There are many celebrities who have launched their careers via social media. It is estimated that around 2 billion people have smartphones connecting to Wi-Fi that continue to expand the marketplace internationally. These high-tech advancements are producing platforms on which business-minded people can build their brand and reach a targeted or broader audience.

Facebook has over 1.71 billion active users

Flickr has over 110 million active users

Google has over 2.2 billion active users

Google + has over 100 million active users

LinkedIn has over 450 million active users

Instagram has over 500 million active users

Periscope has over 10 million active users

Pinterest has over 110 million active users

Reddit has over 235 million active users

Snapchat has over 100 million active users

Tumblr has around 30-50 million active users

Twitter has over 313 million active users

Ustream has over 80 million active users

Vimeo has over 100 million active users

WordPress has over 409 million active users

YouTube has over 1 billion active users

This will be a movement worth celebrating, join the movement ~ Pastor Richie Patterson, Kind Culture

SOCIAL MEDIA

There are many key social media sites that you should be connected to.

Facebook was created in 2004 to allow users to create personal profiles so that friends and associates can find and connect with one another. It also allows people to associate by groups and interests. Users post status updates or thoughts, photos, and locations to those welcomed as friends.
- Facebook Live allows Facebook users to add live video to their feed so that their followers can watch. While the video is playing, followers may comment or react to the videos. Users even can subscribe to a person so that whenever they go live, a notification will appear on their mobile device.

Flickr is an online video and photo hosting platform that allows users to store and access their media and share it to blogs and websites.

Google + is offered by Google. It joins together all the things that you currently do on Google, and adds social functions like posting status updates, creating circles of friends, as well as, finds information that is linked with your interests. You can hang out with people via free video chat or group messaging, and photos can be uploaded instantly.

Instagram is a free service that allows you to share photos from your mobile phone and links to your social media. It was purchased by Facebook and integrates seamlessly with it. The user links together photos and videos and creates a story that can be shared or saved. With drawing tools and other editing features, the user has many options of how to share their media content.

LinkedIn is a social media site for business professionals. Business colleagues' network with each other and allow customers to connect and leave referrals. Users create profiles, which are detailed résumés. There are also additional applications that you can use to expand your profile.

Pinterest is a virtual pinboard that allows users to organize and share photos of images found on the Internet. It is used to aggregate images that you think are relevant to your life or event. Users can browse pinboards of other Pinterest users so that ideas are freely shared.

Reddit is a social news and entertainment site that allows users to submit their information links and text posts. Users vote on an item's popularity. The more popular the posts the higher they are listed on the news feed.

Tumblr is a blogging service with direct links to your social media accounts. You can post all types of information and media with text updates. People can follow your blogs, or you can restrict who can see your blogs

Twitter is a micro-blogging social media site. Users can send messages to one another known as "tweets". Users follow others and grow their network. Users can establish hash tags, retweet other people's messages, and mention other users. Periscope is a live video streaming mobile app purchased by Twitter in 2015. It was game changer for Twitter as millions of people went live from their smartphones to the entire world.

Vimeo is a video sharing platform. Primarily targeted as a service to video and animation professionals. Users offer constructive comments on videos and can rate the videos.

WordPress is an open source website creation tool that offers blogging capabilities and website content management. With its templates, users can quickly construct an attractive website or blog.

YouTube is a social media site that shares video. While users can subscribe to channels, one can search the database and find any video on the site. Keywords are used to grant relevance to one's videos. Videos go viral by having an increasing number of views.

Sell the problem you solve not the product ~unknown

People don't buy what you do, they buy why you do it ~Simon Sinek

SOCIAL MEDIA

List the top three sites you use

_____   _____   _____

LIST 20 people who can like and share what you post on social media.

1. _____   11. _____

2. _____   12. _____

3. _____   13. _____

4. _____   14. _____

5. _____   15. _____

6. _____   16. _____

7. _____   17. _____

8. _____   18. _____

9. _____   19. _____

10. _____   20. _____

Your sphere of influence is greater than you think. Use It!!! ~ +Robbin Hargrove

USING YOUR SPHERE OF INFLUENCE

1. Create a Facebook business page
2. Use your Logo that represents your business (or picture of type of business)
3. Give the overview of your business
   a. Purpose
      i. Problems your business solves
      ii. Audience
4. Post pictures of work you've done
   a. Include events your business was a part of
   b. Action shots (fun pictures)
5. Take the 20 people from the previous page and share this page with them. Get them to like and say something positive about your page.
6. Post on this page at least 5 times a week to start, you want to create a buzz. If you have the time post continuously. This is your baby, if you nurture it will grow.
7. Do a Facebook Live before every event you have and tag your business.

AFTER A WEEK:

What was the most amount of likes you received? _____

If you did a Facebook Live, how many views did you get? _____

What were some of the comments received from those who liked your page?

_____

_____

_____

_____

_____

_____

Review the positive comments made on your business page. Take one word and use it to draw viewers, passerby-ers, scrollers, and onlookers. Do not forget to thank everyone who liked or shared your page.

One who solves problems gets paid. ~ unknown

WHAT IS AN EIN?

Employer identification Number – this is the Social Security number for your business. This number is often referred to as your Tax ID number.

Regardless of the type of business you are looking to start, an EIN number is required. If you are in business and have no employees an EIN number is required. EINs are used by employers, sole proprietors, corporations, partnerships, non-profit organizations, trusts and estates, government agencies, certain individuals and other business entities.

Sole Proprietor, LLCs, L.L.C.

Individual Ownership, no distinction between owner and business. The owner is merely responsible for business whether is rises. A person is not personally liable for the debts of the LLC. A sole proprietor would be liable for the debts incurred by the business.

Corporations, INC

A corporation is an organization, usually a group of people or a company. It is authorized by the state to act as a single entity (legally a person) and recognized as such in law for certain purposes. Corporations may vary but are usually governed by law of the authority where they are appointed by whether they can issue stock or not, or by whether they are formed to make a profit or not. A corporation sole is a legal entity consisting of a single ("sole") incorporated office, occupied by a single ("sole") natural person. Corps can issue stock, those that own stock are often called shareholders, the company can be brought out by those holding majority.

Partnerships

A partnership is a plan where parties agree go into a joint business venture to cooperate to forward their common interests. Persons in a partnership may be individuals, businesses, interest-based organizations, schools, governments or combinations. Organizations may collaborate to broaden reach and benefit from each other achieving their mission. Most partnerships are governed by a contract.

Non-Profit 501(c)(3)

A non-profit organization can vary in different types foundations, churches, community centers, clinic, afterschool programs, homeless shelters, animal shelters to name a few. They are set in place to better the community in which it resides. They can have donors who receive a tax deduction for donations.

Trust, Wills, Estates

A trust is a three-party relationship in which the first known as the settlor who normally has property(estate), grants the second known as the trustee to govern the affairs of this property. For the benefit of the third person the beneficiary. A will normally come into place where the first person dies, and this sheet of paper is counted as a legal document as to how the first person would like the rest of their affairs carried out being, they are no longer alive.

Integrity is doing what's right even when no one else is watching. – C.S Lewis

INC VS LLC

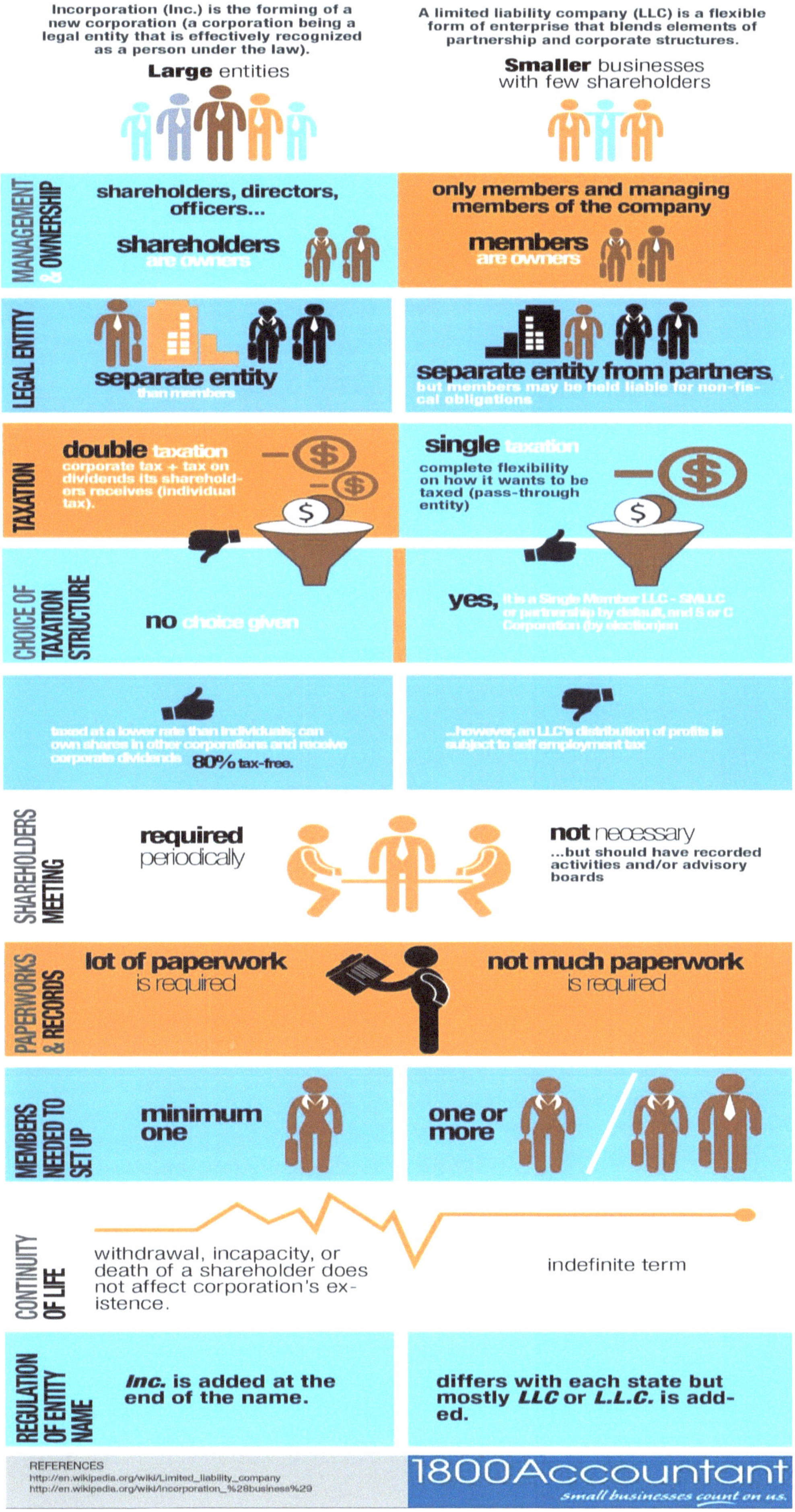

Incorporation (Inc.) is the forming of a new corporation (a corporation being a legal entity that is effectively recognized as a person under the law).
Large entities
A limited liability company (LLC) is a flexible form of enterprise that blends elements of partnership and corporate structures.
Smaller businesses with few shareholders
MANAGEMENT & OWNERSHIP
shareholders, directors, officers...
shareholders are owners
only members and managing members of the company
members are owners
LEGAL ENTITY
separate entity than members
separate entity from partners,
but members may be held liable for non-fiscal obligations
TAXATION
double taxation
corporate tax + tax on dividends its shareholders receives (individual tax).
single taxation
complete flexibility on how it wants to be taxed (pass-through entity)
CHOICE OF TAXATION STRUCTURE
no choice given
yes, it is a Single Member LLC - SMLLC or partnership by default, and S or C Corporation (by election)an
taxed at a lower rate than individuals; can own shares in other corporations and receive corporate dividends 80% tax-free.
...however, an LLC's distribution of profits is subject to self employment tax
SHAREHOLDERS MEETING
required periodically
not necessary
...but should have recorded activities and/or advisory boards
PAPERWORKS & RECORDS
lot of paperwork is required
not much paperwork is required
MEMBERS NEEDED TO SET UP
minimum one
one or more
CONTINUITY OF LIFE
withdrawal, incapacity, or death of a shareholder does not affect corporation's existence.
indefinite term
REGULATION OF ENTITY NAME
Inc. is added at the end of the name.
differs with each state but mostly LLC or L.L.C. is added.
REFERENCES
http://en.wikipedia.org/wiki/Limited_liability_company
http://en.wikipedia.org/wiki/Incorporation_%28business%29
1800Accountant
small businesses count on us.

http://bobbyfinance.com/incorporated-vs-limited-liability-company-infographic/

EIN SAMPLE APPLICATIONS

LIMITED LIABILITY COMPANY

Legal Information

Legal Name of the LLC

Does the LLC have a DBA?   ● No   ○ Yes

Number of members in the LLC   [1]

Select the Tax classification of the LLC:

- ● Individual/Partnership: Not taxed as a separate entity from owner(s).
- ○ S-Corporation: Planning to elect an S-Corporation tax structure.
- ○ Corporation: LLC is planning to elect a Corporation tax structure.

In which state the LLC was incorporated?   [Select a State ▾]

▸ SOLE PROPRIETOR / INDIVIDUAL

Owner Information

First Name

Middle Name (optional)   [Optional]

Last Name

Title   [Please Select ▾]

Social Security Number _Why do we need this?_   [123-45-6789] 🔒

POPULAR BUSINESSES

These are the most popular businesses used to file EINs*

*Based on 2018 reviews, the most popular businesses used to file legal paperwork were these 8 businesses.

Henry Ford summed it up best, If I had asked people what they wanted they would have said a faster horse – Simon Sinek

21

Fees

Fees are going to be included when considering filing paperwork to start your business. There are many agencies to consider. Narrowing down the best one depends on you the potential business owner. To assist in narrowing down your choice, there are a few things to look for in a company that's going to put together your paperwork. Here are some factors:

- ANNUAL COMPLIANCE – Starting at $100 - There are fees associated with keeping your business running every year and operating in full operation according to the IRS

- EMPLOYER IDENTIFICATION NUMBER REGISTRATION – Starting at $75 - There is *no fee* to file with the IRS, however if you are requiring additional services to file required paperwork.

- ORDER PROCESSING TIME – Starting at $50 - Putting all papers together Articles of Operation, EIN number, and other important documents filed with the state. There are fees required for normal 4-5 weeks, to have expedited service the fee will be more.

- OPERATING AGREEMENT – Starting at $350 - This agreement allows you the business owner to set guidelines for governing your business (LLC) oppose to following out state laws for the type of business you are in. You the owner will be able to define specific roles of the management staff. If by chance a situation arises you can refer to this agreement.

- REGISTERED AGENT – Starting At $100 - A registered agent is hired during the start of the business. There duties are to make sure all-important paperwork; Articles of operation, and all necessary compliance paperwork get to the owner and have filed by all due dates. Registered Agents are hired to ensure every business operated in due process. Due process states that before a lawsuit or other legal action can move forward in the courts, all parties in the lawsuit must be properly notified. Registered agents serve to ensure your business can be properly notified, should it be involved in a lawsuit.

The companies listed on prior page have packages and discounts available.

If you think compliance is expensive, try noncompliance.
-Former U.S. Deputy Attorney Gen. Paul McNulty

"The way to get started is to quit talking and begin doing." ~Walt Disney

The individual has always had to struggle to keep from being overwhelmed by the tribe. If you try it, you will feel lonely often, and sometimes frightened. But no price is too high to pay for the privilege of owning yourself.

~FRIEDRICH NIETZCHE

www.ingramcontent.com/pod-product-compliance
Lightning Source LLC
Chambersburg PA
CBHW041310180526
45172CB00003B/1039